100 facts
Coral Reef

100 facts
Coral Reef

Camilla de la Bedoyere

Consultant: Steve Parker

Miles Kelly

First published in 2010 by Miles Kelly Publishing Ltd
Harding's Barn, Bardfield End Green, Thaxted, Essex, CM6 3PX

2 4 6 8 10 9 7 5 3

Editorial Director: Belinda Gallagher
Art Director: Jo Brewer
Managing Editor: Rosie McGuire
Assistant Editor: Claire Philip
Volume Designer: Andrea Slane
Image Manager: Liberty Newton
Indexer: Gill Lee
Production Manager: Elizabeth Brunwin
Reprographics: Stephan Davis, Jennifer Hunt, Ian Paulyn

ISBN 978-1-84810-272-9

Printed in China

British Library Cataloguing-in-Publication Data
A catalogue record for this book is available from the British Library

ACKNOWLEDGEMENTS
The publishers would like to thank the following artists
who have contributed to this book:

Mike Foster (Maltings Partnership), Ian Jackson,
Andrea Morandi, Mike Saunders

All other artworks are from the Miles Kelly Artwork Bank

The publishers would like to thank the following sources
for the use of their photographs:

t = top, b = bottom, l = left, r = right, c = centre

Cover: Georgette Douwma/Getty Images
Pages 6–7 Georgette Douwma/Science Photo Library; 8(bl) Paul Kay/Photolibrary.com,
(tr) Planetobserver/Science Photo Library; 9 WaterFrame/Alamy; 10 Jeff Rotman/Naturepl.com;
14 Tom McHugh/Science Photo Library; 15(t) Jouke van der Meer/iStockphoto.com; 16 (clockwise from top right)
Vintrom/Dreamstime.com, Frhojdysz/Dreamstime.com, Dave Bluck/iStockphoto.com; 17 (clockwise from top right)
Anders Nygren/iStockphoto.com, Brento/Dreamstime.com, Ajalber/Dreamstime.com; 18(b) Frans Lanting/Corbis;
19 Vladimir Ovchinnikov/Fotolia.com; 22 Paul Kay/Photolibrary.com; 23(tr) khz/Fotolia.com;
24(b) Mike Parry/Minden Pictures/FLPA; 25(bl) TSWinner/iStockphoto.com,(tr) Gary Bell/OceanwideImages.com;
27(t) Peter Schinck/Fotolia.com; 27 Allister Clark/iStockphoto.com; 28 Monica & Michael Sweet/Photolibrary.com;
29 Dana Edmunds/Photolibrary.com; 30(c) Goodolga/Dreamstime.com, (b) Surub/Dreamstime.com; 31(tl) cbpix/Fotolia.com;
36–37 Juniors Bildarchiv/Photolibrary.com; 36(br) Johnandersonphoto/Dreamstime.com; 37(br) Olga Khoroshunova/iStockphoto.com;
38(t) Donsimon/Dreamstime.com, (b) Wolfgang Poelzer/Photolibrary.com; 39 Jurgen Freund/Naturepl.com; 40 Stephen Frink/Corbis;
41 Jeff Hunter/Getty; 42(t) Stephankerkhofs/Dreamstime.com, (b) Djmattaar/Dreamstime.com; 43 Georgette Douwma/Naturepl.com;
44 Georgette Douwma/Science Photo Library; 45 Kurt Amsler/Ardea.com; 46 Franco Banfi/Photolibrary.com;
47(t) NASA, (r) Reinhard Dirscherl/Photolibrary.com

All other photographs are from:
Corel, digitalSTOCK, digitalvision, ImageState, iStockphoto.com, PhotoDisc

Every effort has been made to acknowledge the source and copyright holder of each picture.
Miles Kelly Publishing apologises for any unintentional errors or omissions.

Made with paper from a sustainable forest

www.mileskelly.net
info@mileskelly.net

www.factsforprojects.com
The one-stop homework helper —
pictures, facts, videos, projects and more

www.coralcay.org

The publishers would like to thank Coral Cay
Conservation for their help in compiling this book.

Contents

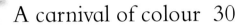

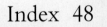

Rainforests of the sea

1 Beautiful coral reefs lie beneath the sparkling surfaces of sapphire-blue seas. Although they only take up a tiny amount of space in the world's oceans, coral reefs contain more than one-quarter of all types of sea creatures and are home to billions of animals and plants. Coral reefs are among the Earth's most precious places but they are in grave danger of disappearing forever.

◄ Reefs teem with life as fish dart and dash around stone-like coral structures. Panda butterflyfish inhabit reefs in tropical oceans and can grow up to 20 centimetres in length.

What are coral reefs?

2 Coral reefs are ocean habitats (homes) made by the creatures that live inside them. Tiny coral animals called polyps live together in huge numbers, known as colonies. They can grow for thousands of years, building reefs that can measure more than 2000 kilometres long.

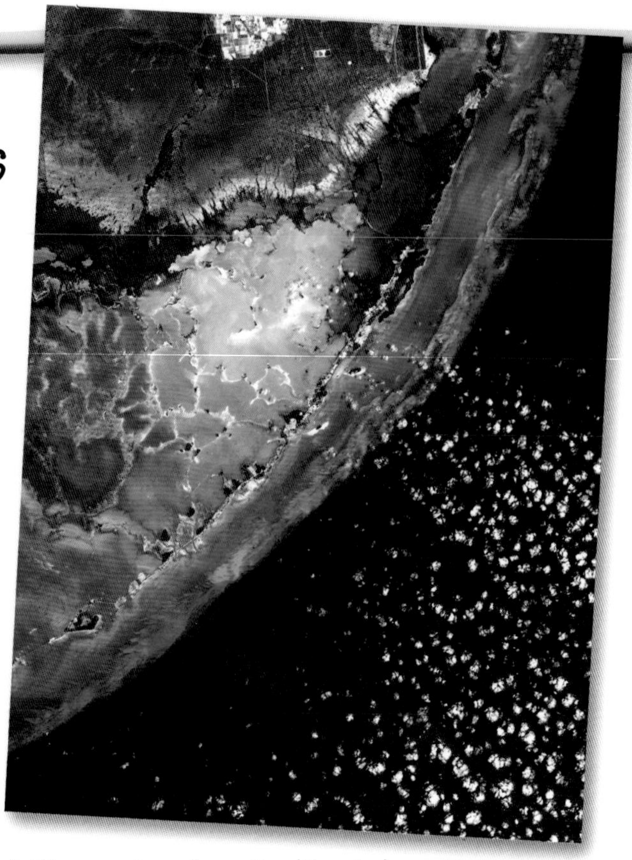

▲ The coral reefs in the Florida Keys National Marine Sanctuary are so vast they can be seen from space.

3 Reefs are home to many animals and plants. Together, the reef and all the things living in it make up an ecosystem. Coral reefs are some of the most varied ecosystems in the world, and are thriving, colourful places that burst with life.

◄ Sea anemones attach themselves to the reef structure and fish hide away in the many nooks and crannies.

CORAL REEF KEY

1 White-spotted rose anemone
2 Club-tipped anemone
3 Gopher rockfish

4 It is not only coral polyps that help a reef to grow. Polyps provide the framework of a reef, but other living things add to the structure. Some marine (sea) organisms, such as sponges and sea cucumbers, have a hard substance called silicon in their skeletons. When they die, their skeletons add to the coral reef.

5 Land-living animals and plants also depend on reefs. In shallow water, plants take root in the mud and sand that collects around a reef. Mangrove trees and sea grasses grow here – the spaces around their roots make good places for animals, such as crabs, to hide. Long-legged birds also wade through mud and water, looking for food.

6 Coral reefs have been around for at least 230 million years. They are among the oldest ecosystems in the world. Despite their great age, coral reefs do not appear to have changed very much in this time.

◄ The warm waters around mangrove roots are a perfect place for soft tree corals to grow.

Coral animals

7 Coral polyps are the little animals that build reefs. Their soft bodies are like rubber tubes with an opening at their centre. This is the mouth, which is surrounded by rows of tentacles. Each tentacle is equipped with stingers called cnidocytes (say nido-sites).

8 Coral polyps have a special relationship with tiny life-forms called zooxanthellae (say zoo-zan-thell-ee). These are plant-like algae that live inside a polyp's body, providing it with some of the food it needs to grow. In return, the polyps provide the algae with a safe place to live. Zooxanthellae need sunlight to survive, so they live inside a polyp's tentacles, where light can reach them.

◄ Cup corals are a non reef-building species that use their tentacles to catch prey. Coral polyps are in the same animal family as jellyfish and sea anemones, and are known as 'cnidarians' (say nid-air-ee-ans).

9 Sea animals do not always go looking for food. Coral polyps cannot move around, so they grab whatever food comes their way, using their tentacles. When a tentacle touches something edible, a tiny stinger springs out and pierces the prey's skin. The tentacles draw the prey into the polyp's mouth.

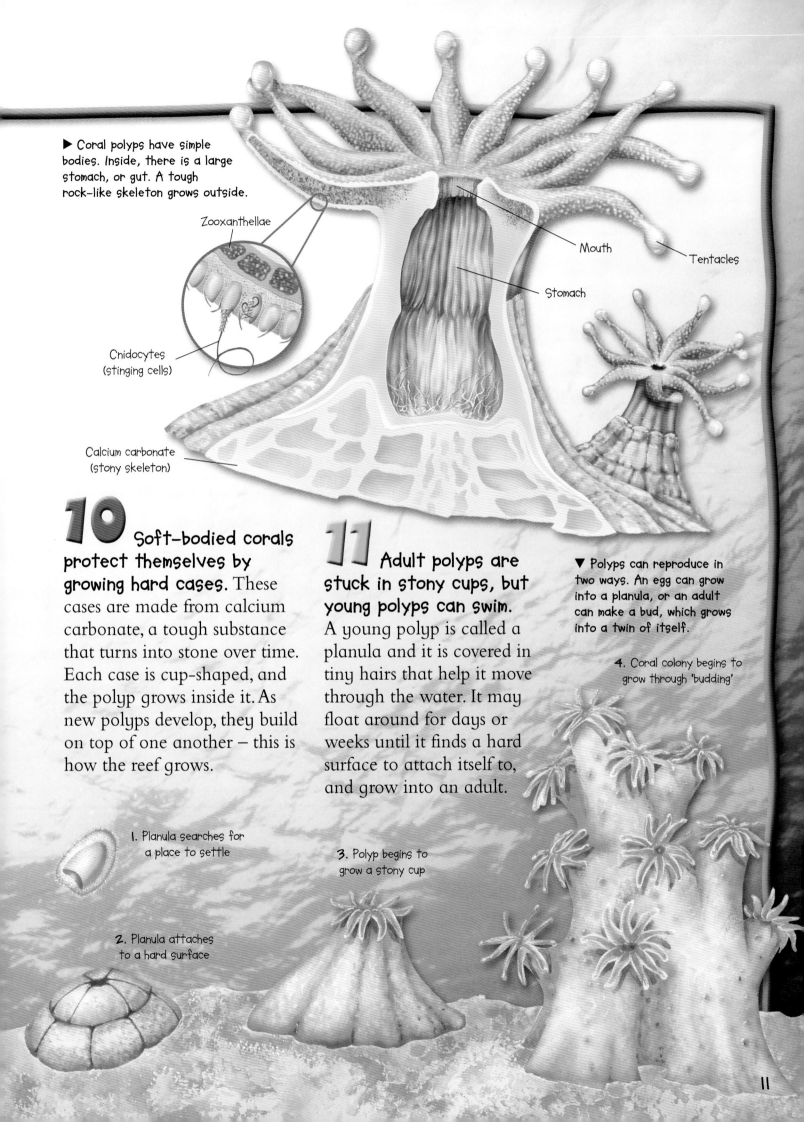

▶ Coral polyps have simple bodies. Inside, there is a large stomach, or gut. A tough rock-like skeleton grows outside.

Zooxanthellae

Chidocytes (stinging cells)

Calcium carbonate (stony skeleton)

Mouth

Stomach

Tentacles

10
Soft-bodied corals protect themselves by growing hard cases. These cases are made from calcium carbonate, a tough substance that turns into stone over time. Each case is cup-shaped, and the polyp grows inside it. As new polyps develop, they build on top of one another – this is how the reef grows.

11
Adult polyps are stuck in stony cups, but young polyps can swim. A young polyp is called a planula and it is covered in tiny hairs that help it move through the water. It may float around for days or weeks until it finds a hard surface to attach itself to, and grow into an adult.

▼ Polyps can reproduce in two ways. An egg can grow into a planula, or an adult can make a bud, which grows into a twin of itself.

4. Coral colony begins to grow through 'budding'

1. Planula searches for a place to settle

3. Polyp begins to grow a stony cup

2. Planula attaches to a hard surface

Hard and soft

12 There are two main types of coral — hard coral and soft coral. Hard coral polyps are reef-builders — they use calcium carbonate to build strong structures around themselves. Soft corals are bendy, and often live alongside their stony cousins.

13 Warm water reefs can look like colourful gardens. Corals grow in many unusual shapes, appearing like bushes, trees and mushrooms. The shape of coral depends upon the type of polyp that lives within it, and its position on the reef.

14 Some corals are easy to identify because they look just like their name. Brain corals, for example, look like brains. They grow very slowly and can reach the size of a boulder. Staghorn coral is one of the fastest-growing types, and it is an important reef-builder, especially in shallow waters. Each staghorn polyp can live for around ten years, and will not reproduce until it reaches at least three years old.

▼ Corals are different shapes and sizes. The way each coral grows depends on the type of polyps that live inside the rocky structures.

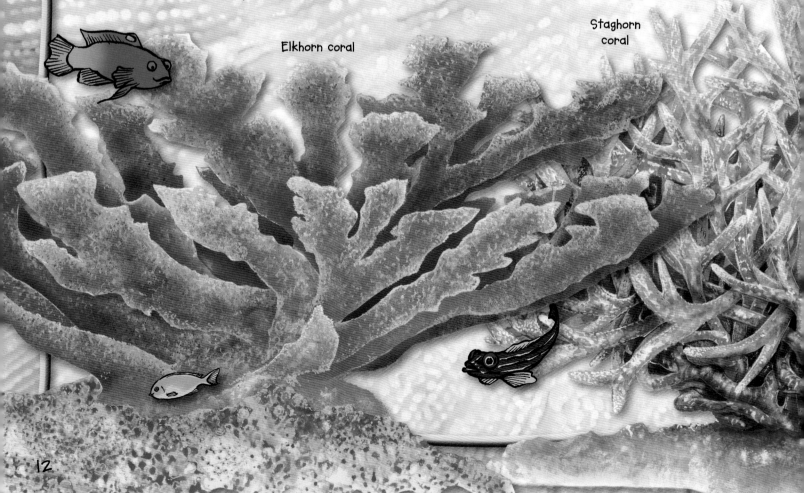

Elkhorn coral

Staghorn coral

Brain coral

Mushroom coral

15 Not all coral polyps live together in colonies. Some types live alone in the Southern Ocean, near the Antarctic, where temperatures rarely creep above a chilly 6°C. Little is known about solitary corals, but it is thought they are sensitive to water temperature.

Sea fan

Lettuce coral

Sea whip

Soft tree coral

Ancient reefs

QUIZ

If a porites coral is 1000 years old, and it has grown one centimetre every year, how big is it? How big will it be when it is 2000 years old?

Answers:
1000 centimetres in 1000 years and 2000 centimetres in 2000 years.

16 Corals haven't changed much over the last few hundred million years. Coral polyps that lived at the same time as the dinosaurs, around 100 million years ago, are very similar to those alive today. The oldest coral on the Great Barrier Reef, Australia, is called porites. It is around 1000 years old.

17 Throughout time, extinctions (the dying out of a particular type of animal or plant) have occurred. The largest mass extinction happened around 250 million years ago. Many reef-building corals died out at this time, to be replaced by other types that evolved thousands, or even millions, of years later.

▼ This is how a coral reef might have looked around 390 million years ago.

CORAL REEF KEY

(1) Giant horn corals grew to one metre long

(2) Shelled creatures with tentacles are related to today's octopuses

(3) Crinoids grew long stems and a ring of feathery 'arms' around their mouths

(4) Corals grew in large colonies, as they still do today

▲ Stromatolite mounds are still growing today in Brazil, Mexico and Western Australia.

18 **The oldest reefs were laid down more than 500 million years ago.** They were made of mounds, called stromatolites, that were created by tiny life-forms called cyanobacteria. Over millions of years, the mounds joined together to make ancient reefs.

▲ Coral colonies can harden and turn into stone over time. They are known as fossils.

19 **Over millions of years, coral reefs can turn into a type of stone, called limestone.** Scientists know about extinct reef animals by looking at limestones and the preserved remains of animals within them. These remains are called fossils and scientists can study them to understand how the Earth, animals and plants have changed over time.

20 **The sites of some ancient coral reefs have become land.** The Marshall Islands lie in the centre of the Pacific Ocean, near the Equator (the midway point between the North and South poles). The islands are made of limestone, and when scientists drilled deep down into the rock, they discovered that the oldest parts of the reefs there grew 50 million years ago.

Where in the world?

21 Warm water coral reefs may be packed with life, but they only cover around 284,000 square kilometres of the Earth's surface. If you put them all together, they would still only take up the same room as a small country, such as New Zealand.

▲ Blue-spotted stingrays hunt their prey among the Red Sea corals.

22 The Coral Triangle is an enormous region that stretches across the seas around Indonesia, Malaysia and Papua New Guinea. It contains some of the world's most precious reefs, and is home to 3000 species of fish and 20 species of mammals, including dugongs, whales and dolphins.

23 Coral polyps are choosy about where they grow. This is because the zooxanthellae that live with them need warmth and light to turn the sun's energy into food. They are most likely to grow in seas and oceans within a region called the tropics, which is between the Tropic of Cancer and the Tropic of Capricorn.

◄ Damselfish and sea anemones are just two of the many animals that live on the Indian Ocean reefs.

Tropic of Cancer

RED SEA

Coral Triangle

Equator

INDIAN OCEAN

Gre Barr Ree

Tropic of Capricorn

◄ A pink porcelain crab rests on a hard coral near Malaysia, in the Coral Triangle.

QUIZ

Which of these are oceans, and which are seas?

Atlantic   Mediterranean
Caribbean   Indian
Pacific   Coral

Answers:
Atlantic, Pacific and Indian are oceans. Caribbean, Mediterranean and Coral are seas.

24 **Dirty water is no good to coral polyps.** They prefer clear water, without the tiny particles of dirt, mud or sand that prevent light from reaching the seabed. Reefs don't grow near river mouths, or in areas where dirt is washed from the land into the sea. Polyps are even fussy about the amount of salt dissolved in the ocean water around them.

◀ Pygmy seahorses live in the warm coral waters of the western Pacific Ocean.

◀ The Hawaiian reef fish Humuhumunukunukuapua'a is a type of triggerfish, and makes pig-like snorting sounds if threatened.

ATLANTIC OCEAN

Hawaiian reefs

PACIFIC OCEAN

CARIBBEAN SEA

Mesoamerican Reef

25 **Sunlight cannot pass through water as easily as it can pass through air.** As zooxanthellae need light, their coral polyps only grow in water with a maximum depth of around 11 metres – although this varies depending on how clean the water is. This explains why warm water coral reefs grow near the land, where the water is shallow.

CORAL SEA

▲ The Caribbean reef octopus feeds at night, and eats fish and shelled animals.

◀ Giant clams live in coral reefs around the South Pacific and Indian Oceans.

SOUTHERN OCEAN

Types of reef

26 There are three main types of coral reef. Fringing reefs are the most common. They grow on the edges of land that are underwater, often with little or no gap in between the reef and dry land. Barrier reefs also grow where land meets the ocean, but they are separated from the land by a stretch of water, called a lagoon. Atolls are circular reefs with a lagoon in the centre.

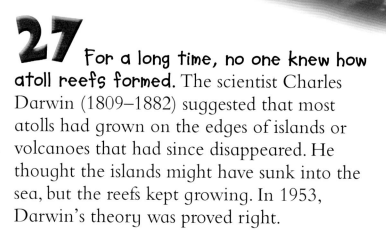

① When coral grows around an island's coasts, a fringing reef develops.

27 For a long time, no one knew how atoll reefs formed. The scientist Charles Darwin (1809–1882) suggested that most atolls had grown on the edges of islands or volcanoes that had since disappeared. He thought the islands might have sunk into the sea, but the reefs kept growing. In 1953, Darwin's theory was proved right.

② The island drops, or the sea rises, and the coral becomes a barrier reef.

28 Patch reefs form in shallow water and their tops are only visible at low tide. They are usually round or oval in shape and their outer edges are ringed by coral sand leading to beds of sea grass.

29 Bank reefs often grow in lines, or in semi-circles. They have large buttress zones (the area of a reef that faces the sea) with ridges of tough coral that grow out into it. Elkhorn coral grows here because it is able to withstand strong waves.

30 The Maldives are coral islands in the Indian Ocean. As they are built from coral, most land is no more than 1.5 metres above sea level. People have been living in the Maldives for more than 2000 years. There is little soil on the islands so few plants, other than coconut palms, grow well. Local people have survived by fishing and, more recently from tourism.

3 When there is no longer any sign of the island the reef is called an atoll.

Reef

Lagoon

Zones of the reef

31 Coral reefs can grow so large that it is possible to see them from outer space. Yet it is only the outer parts of a reef that are alive. The parts beneath the surface are dead, made up from the billions of stony cups that once housed living coral polyps.

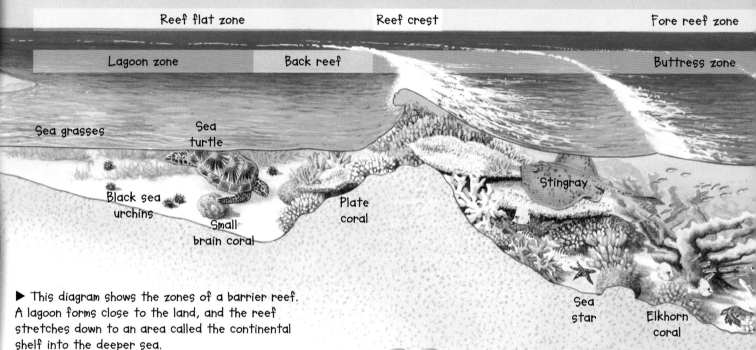

Reef flat zone · Reef crest · Fore reef zone
Lagoon zone · Back reef · Buttress zone

Sea grasses · Sea turtle · Black sea urchins · Small brain coral · Plate coral · Stingray · Sea star · Elkhorn coral

▶ This diagram shows the zones of a barrier reef. A lagoon forms close to the land, and the reef stretches down to an area called the continental shelf into the deeper sea.

32 The part of a reef that is closest to land is called a reef flat. It is difficult for polyps to grow well here because of the effect of the tides, which may leave the coral exposed to air for too long, and because the water can become too salty. The reef flat is home to many types of animals that scuttle around between sea grasses, dig into the soft mud, or stick to the old, dead stony structures.

33 Most corals grow on the sides of the reef that face the sea and wind. This area is known as the fore reef and it is warmed by ocean currents. The corals here grow upwards and outwards, building up layers over thousands of years. Below the fore reef is a collection of old coral material that has broken off and fallen to the seafloor. The highest part of the fore reef is the crest – the polyps that live here must be able to survive strong waves and winds.

34 **The fore reef is divided into three parts.** At the bottom, plate-shaped corals grow where there is less light. As they grow they spread out to reach the sunlight. Nearby, fan corals are stretched in front of the water currents that flow towards them. In the middle part larger, mound-shaped corals grow and near the crest, long-fingered strong corals, such as staghorn, appear.

35 **Further out to sea, a reef develops a buttress zone.** Here, large spurs or clumps of coral grow, breaking up the waves and absorbing some of their impact before they hit the rest of the reef. This is the area where sharks and barracudas are most likely to swim. Beyond the buttress zone lies the reef wall, which forms in a deeper part of the sea.

Deep reef zone

Bottlenose dolphins

Sea goldies

Sea whip

Sea fan

Maze coral

Tube sponge

Butterfly fish

Dead coral bedrock

Lettuce coral

Star coral

Wobbegong shark

Barracudas

Whitetip reef shark

I DON'T BELIEVE IT!

Coral reefs are very slow growers. A reef can grow about 10 centimetres a year if the conditions are just right – how much have you grown in the last year?

21

Cold water corals

36 In the cold, dark ocean waters, coral reefs lay hidden for thousands of years. A few of these deep sea reefs were found about 250 years ago, but it has recently been discovered that in fact, there are more cold water reefs than warm water ones.

BIG BUILDERS

Find out about some other animal architects. Use the Internet or the library to discover how bees, termites and sociable weaver birds work together to build structures.

▼ A cold water reef grows in the chilly waters north of Scotland. Visible are dead man's fingers coral (1), a jewel anemone (2) and a common sea urchin (3).

37 Cold water corals live in waters between 200 and 1500 metres deep. The largest cold water coral reef is more than 40 kilometres long and up to 3 kilometres wide. Just like warm water corals, these deep sea reefs are home to a large range of animals, many of which live nowhere else on Earth.

38 Deep sea coral polyps don't have zooxanthellae, so they don't need sunlight to survive. They have to get all their food by feeding on tiny animals, called zooplankton, that drift past them. They catch these creatures with their tentacles and poison stingers, and draw them into their mouths.

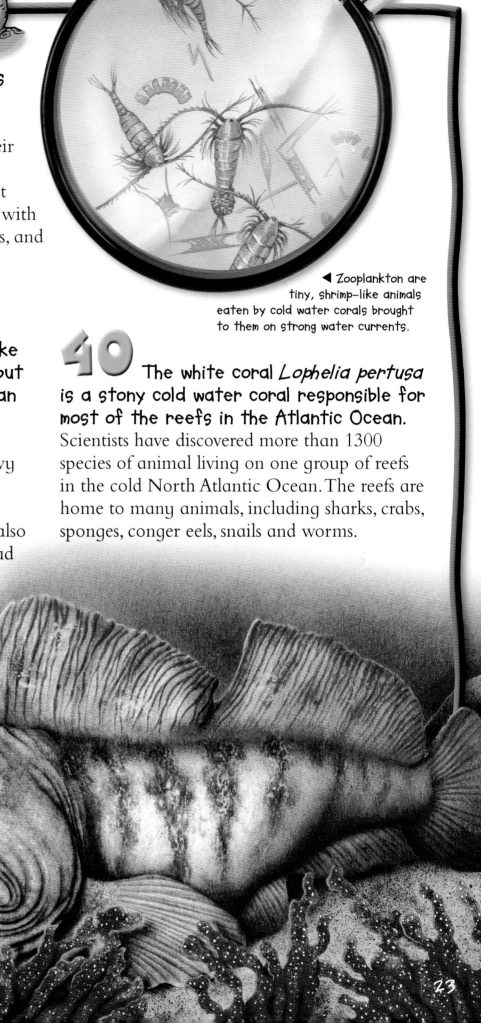

◄ Zooplankton are tiny, shrimp-like animals eaten by cold water corals brought to them on strong water currents.

39 Cold water corals take thousands of years to grow, but they are being destroyed at an alarming rate. Scientists believe most of the damage is caused by trawling, a type of fishing. A heavy net is pulled over, or near, the sea floor by a boat. As it is dragged along the net catches fish, but it also damages coral and churns up mud and pollution.

40 The white coral *Lophelia pertusa* is a stony cold water coral responsible for most of the reefs in the Atlantic Ocean. Scientists have discovered more than 1300 species of animal living on one group of reefs in the cold North Atlantic Ocean. The reefs are home to many animals, including sharks, crabs, sponges, conger eels, snails and worms.

▼ Wolf-fish have powerful jaws, which they use to eat crabs and shelled animals that live around cold water corals.

The Great Barrier Reef

41 The Great Barrier Reef, on the north-east coast of Australia, is possibly the largest structure ever built by animals. It covers an area of the Coral Sea that extends for more than 2000 kilometres and it took around 18 million years for the reef to grow to this enormous size.

42 It may look like one giant structure, but the Great Barrier Reef is really made up of around 3000 smaller reefs and 1000 islands. Although coral has grown in this region for millions of years the barrier reef only formed at the end of the last Ice Age, around 10,000 years ago.

◄ When leafy seadragons hide among seaweed they become almost invisible.

43 The Great Barrier Reef was not studied by scientists until the 18th century. British explorer James Cook (1728–1779) sailed his ship, HMS *Endeavour*, onto the reef in June 1770, and his crew had to spend six weeks repairing the damage to their craft. Ever since, explorers and scientists have been studying the structure of the reef and its wildlife.

▼ Dugongs are air-breathing animals that swim around the reef, grazing on sea grasses.

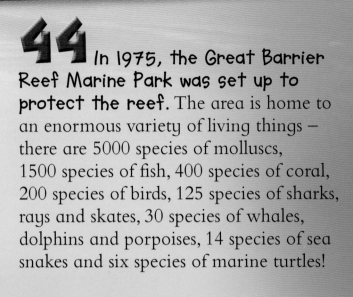

44 In 1975, the Great Barrier Reef Marine Park was set up to protect the reef. The area is home to an enormous variety of living things — there are 5000 species of molluscs, 1500 species of fish, 400 species of coral, 200 species of birds, 125 species of sharks, rays and skates, 30 species of whales, dolphins and porpoises, 14 species of sea snakes and six species of marine turtles!

▶ Groups, or shoals, of sweetlips swim around the Great Barrier Reef.

QUIZ

Can you add up all the numbers of species listed in fact 44, from molluscs to turtles? Check your answer with a calculator.

Answer:
5000 + 1500 + 400 + 200 + 125 + 30 + 14 + 6 = 7275.

45 Native people and nearby islanders from the Torres Strait have fished in the Coral Sea for more than 60,000 years. They are known as the Traditional Owners of the Great Barrier Reef. The areas of the reef that they used in the practice of their ancient lifestyles are called the sea country. Traditional Owners work to preserve their ancient connection to the Great Barrier Reef.

◀ Like many sea snakes, olive sea snakes have a poisonous bite.

Caribbean coral

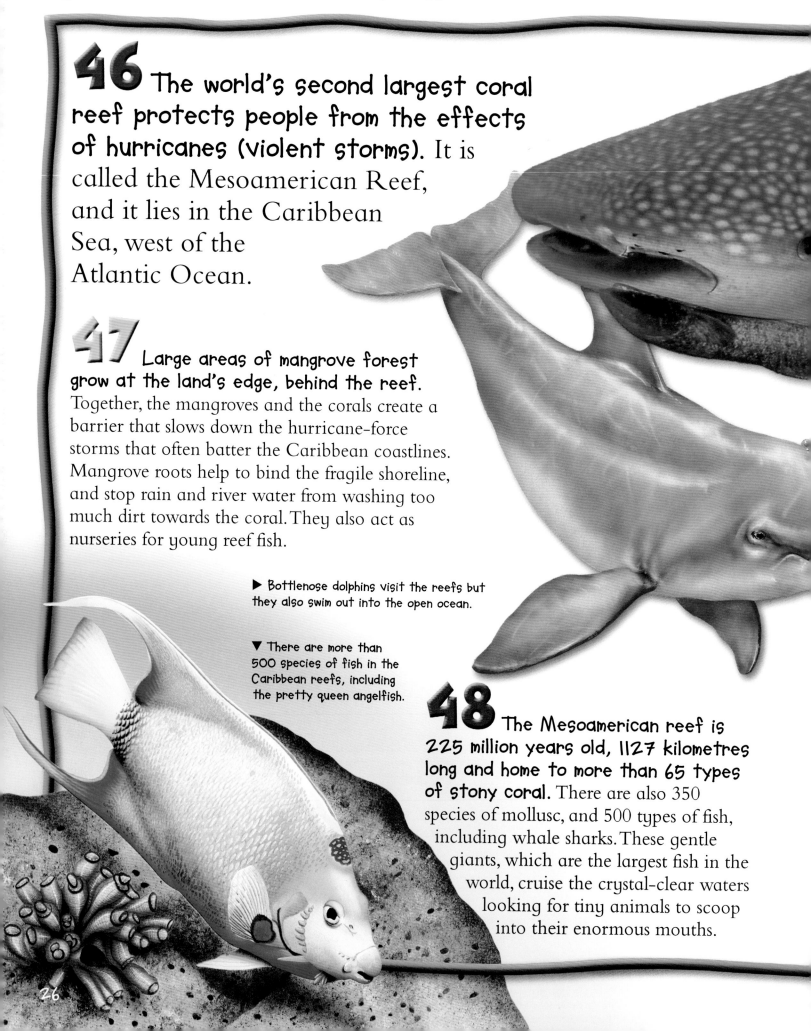

46 The world's second largest coral reef protects people from the effects of hurricanes (violent storms). It is called the Mesoamerican Reef, and it lies in the Caribbean Sea, west of the Atlantic Ocean.

47 Large areas of mangrove forest grow at the land's edge, behind the reef. Together, the mangroves and the corals create a barrier that slows down the hurricane-force storms that often batter the Caribbean coastlines. Mangrove roots help to bind the fragile shoreline, and stop rain and river water from washing too much dirt towards the coral. They also act as nurseries for young reef fish.

▶ Bottlenose dolphins visit the reefs but they also swim out into the open ocean.

▼ There are more than 500 species of fish in the Caribbean reefs, including the pretty queen angelfish.

48 The Mesoamerican reef is 225 million years old, 1127 kilometres long and home to more than 65 types of stony coral. There are also 350 species of mollusc, and 500 types of fish, including whale sharks. These gentle giants, which are the largest fish in the world, cruise the crystal-clear waters looking for tiny animals to scoop into their enormous mouths.

▲ It is thought that whale sharks can live to be 100 years old or more. They eat small fish and krill around reefs and in deep water.

49 Throughout history, people who live near the reef have depended on its fish for food. Many of the people who live in coastal areas in countries such as Belize, Mexico, Honduras and Guatemala have long family traditions of fishing around the reef. They discovered that swarms of fish come together during full moons to mate, and this was the perfect time to catch them in nets.

▲ Tourists enjoy the wildlife spectacle around a reef. They can snorkel, or take a ride in a glass-bottomed boat.

50 Pirates used to hide their ships among the many Caribbean islands that are dotted along the reef. Explorers came too, looking for treasure such as gold and silver, and to set up trading routes. Today, tourists flock to the area to enjoy the exploring this ecosystem and its beautiful coral gardens.

Islands of fire

51 **The coral reefs of Hawaii are unlike any others found on Earth.** They have formed around a string of islands, called an archipelago, that developed when volcanoes erupted in the middle of the Pacific Ocean. Hawaii is about 3200 kilometres from any large land mass, which means these are the world's most isolated group of islands.

52 **Around one-quarter of the animals and plants that live on Hawaiian coral reefs are found nowhere else.** Algae, which are seaweeds, thrive in this area – especially the stony seaweeds that help to bind reefs together and make them stronger. Algae are important because they take carbon dioxide from the air and expel oxygen, the gas that animals such as polyps need to breathe.

▼ Enormous humpback whales use the waters around Hawaii as nurseries. They stay here with their young until it is time to swim north.

I DON'T BELIEVE IT!

Huge humpback whales feed on tiny krill, which are shrimp-like creatures. They don't feed in the winter, so at this time of year the krill have nothing to fear.

▲▶ Hawaiian corals (1) have grown on old lava that has cooled and turned to stone (2).

53 Volcanoes began to erupt in this area around 70 million years ago, and they are still active today. As lava cooled and turned to stone, corals began to grow on their edges. The first polyps must have arrived as free-swimming planulas, probably from other Pacific coral reefs.

55 Around 10,000 endangered humpback whales visit Hawaii every year. They arrive at the warm tropical waters in the winter, after swimming all the way from their feeding grounds in Alaska. While in Hawaii, the whales give birth to their young, and care for them. They can be seen swimming, playing and even battling with one another around the coral reefs.

◀ Green turtles lay their eggs on Hawaiian beaches because the reefs protect them from storms and waves.

54 The islanders of Hawaii set up a marine park in 1967, to protect the reef ecosystem. In 1956 an enormous channel, more than 60 metres wide, was blasted into the coral using dynamite to make way for a new telephone cable. The coral is now protected by law.

◀ A bobtail squid can produce light in its belly, which helps it hunt at night. The light is produced by bacteria that live on the squid.

A carnival of colour

56 Some animals stay on the sea floor, or hide in cracks in the coral reef, but others dart, dive and dazzle their way through the clear waters. Coral reef animals often use the colours of their shells or skins to help them lurk unseen in the shadows, or to warn other animals to stay away. When an animal uses colour to hide, it is said to be camouflaged.

57 Coral fish come in beautiful patterns and brilliant colours. Good looks are important for their survival – red colours appear dark in water, stripes provide camouflage and spots can confuse predators. Blue and yellow fish look bright to us, but they are hidden on the reef. The way sunlight is reflected off coral reefs affects the appearance of blues and yellows, making them blend in with the background.

▲▼ Coral fish come in many different colours and patterns such as the coral trout (top), regal angelfish (middle) and blue tang fish (below).

58 Squid and cuttlefish create flashes of colour. These soft-bodied molluscs can change their colours in an instant to hide or attract prey towards them. They can produce skin colours of red, yellow, orange, brown and black – and can even create patterns, such as zebra stripes, on their skin.

◀ Sea slugs are brightly coloured to warn predators that they are very poisonous.

59 Land slugs are slimy and often dull in colour, but coral reef slugs are bizarre, beautiful animals. Sea slugs, also called nudibranchs, don't have shells, but they do have soft, feathery gills on their backs, which help them to breathe in water. Some nudibranchs are small, but the largest ones can grow to 30 centimetres long.

60 The stripes, spines and bright colours of a lionfish spell danger to other coral creatures. These ocean fish hunt other fish, shrimp and sea anemones. When they are threatened they react with lightning speed. Lionfish have spines on their bodies that carry deadly venom, which they raise and plunge into a predator's flesh.

▼ Lionfish hide among rocks in the daytime, and only come out at night to hunt for food. They have been known to threaten divers.

GO FISH!

Choose your favourite colourful coral fish from this book and copy it onto a large piece of paper or card. Use different materials, such as paints, tissue paper, buttons and foil to show the colours and patterns.

On the attack

61 Animals need energy to survive, and they get that energy from food. Some reef animals graze on seaweeds and corals, but others hunt and kill to feed. Hunting animals are called predators, and their victims are called prey.

▶ When sharks, such as these lemon sharks, sense blood or food they move with speed to attack their prey.

62 Some coral sharks aren't aggressive and divers can feed them by hand. Bull sharks are not so relaxed around humans. They have been known to attack divers and swimmers around reefs. Sharks are drawn to coral reefs because of the thousands of fish on the reef but finding prey is not always easy when there are so many good hiding places.

63 Cone shells look harmless, but their appearance is deceptive. These sea snails crawl around reefs looking for prey such as worms, molluscs and fish. They fire venom-filled darts to paralyze their prey. The dart remains attached to the cone shell, so it can draw its victim back to its body and devour it.

◀ This small animal cannot protect itself from an attack by a deadly cone shell.

64 Sea anemones and jellyfish have stingers to attack their prey, just like their coral cousins. Soft-bodied sea anemones are usually quite small and they stay attached to the sea floor, or coral, and wait for water currents to bring food their way. Jellyfish have tentacles that can stretch for many metres, hanging below their bodies. Jellyfish can swim, or they are carried along by the sea's currents.

65 Mantis shrimps are mighty crustaceans. They punch or spear their prey, using such incredible force and speed that they are regarded as one of the most powerful animals in the world for their size. These small animals are common in Australian coral reefs and parts of the Indo-Pacific reef system.

▼ A blue-ringed octopus is only 20 centimetres long but its saliva contains poison that is strong enough to kill a human.

▲ Box jellyfish have such deadly stings that beaches are often closed in Australia when they are present in the water.

I DON'T BELIEVE IT!
Mantis shrimps are powerful punchers. They surprise their prey by hitting out at speeds of 240 metres per second.

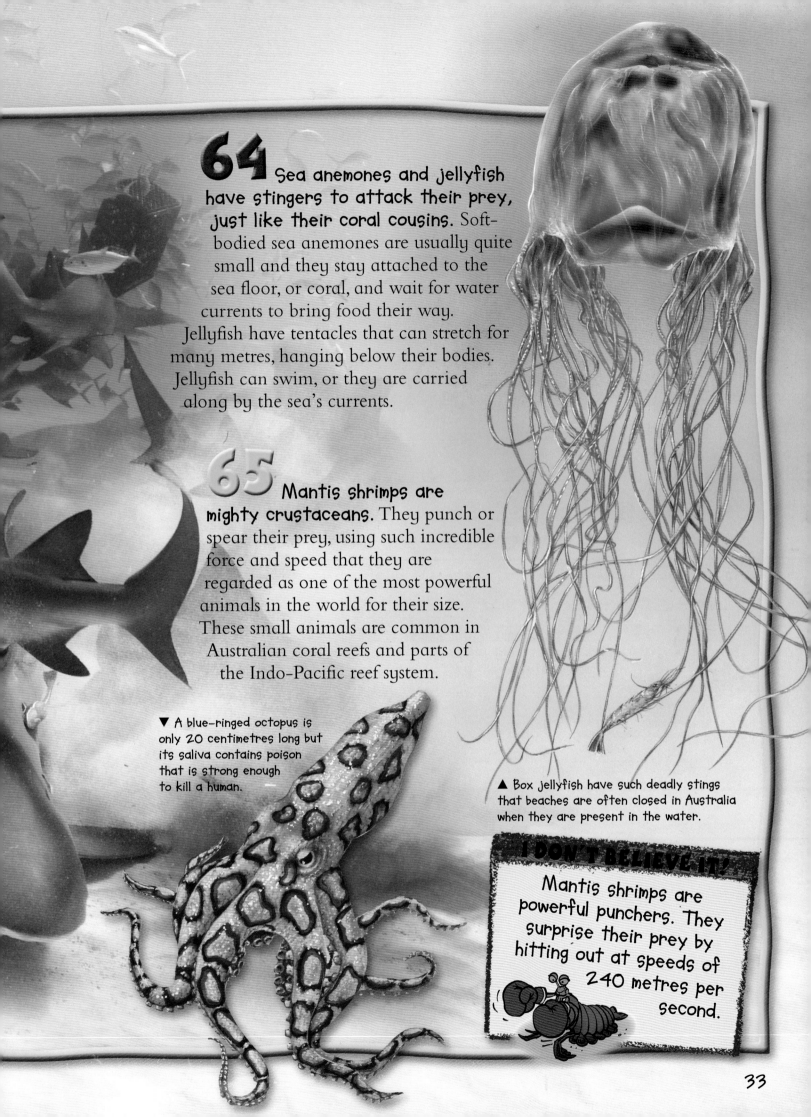

Living together

66 The animals and plants that live on coral reefs need each other to survive. The close relationship between some animals is known as 'symbiosis'. Sometimes these partnerships give benefits to both animals, but at other times one animal gains little.

67 Coral polyps and their zooxanthellae are best buddies. Each zooxanthellae is made of just one cell. Like green plants, zooxanthellae make food using sunlight, water and carbon dioxide – a gas that is in the air. This process is called photosynthesis. The food they make is eaten by the polyps. Because they need sunlight to grow, zooxanthellae live inside a polyp's tentacles where light can reach them.

▼ Clownfish can hide among the stinging tentacles of a sea anemone without getting stung.

▲ Remora fish use other animals – such as this green turtle – to hitch a ride and find food.

I DON'T BELIEVE IT!

Boxer crabs use stinging sea anemones like boxing gloves. They wave them at any predators who get too close!

68 Coral fish dance to tell other reef animals that they are ready to get cleaning. Bluestreak cleaner wrasses feed on irritating parasites that attach themselves to other fishes' bodies, causing them harm. When they are hungry the wrasses dance to attract attention, and the bigger fish queue up to wait for their cleaning services.

▲ A moray eel patiently waits while a wrasse cleans its mouth.

69 Remoras are fish that hitch a ride on sharks, using specially adapted fins that work like sticky suckers. They get carried around the reef without having to spend any energy on swimming, but they may affect sharks' hunting ability by slowing them down. Remoras also latch on to dolphins and turtles.

70 Giant clams also have best buddies that they rely on to survive. These molluscs can grow up to 1.5 metres long and can live for more than 70 years. Zooxanthellae live on the fringes of these animals' enormous shells and provide the clams with nutrients. The clams and the algae need each other to survive, just like coral polyps and their algae.

▼ Hermit crabs depend on other shelled animals for their homes. They find empty shells and move in.

Night on the reef

71 **As the Sun sets over the ocean, coral reefs change.** Polyps emerge from their cups and unfurl their tentacles, producing a range of colours and movements. Creatures that were active in daylight rest in dark crevices, while others emerge to feed in the dark.

72 **Coral animals that come out at night are described as nocturnal.** They often have senses that help them to detect movement, light, sound and chemicals in the inky-blue seas. Octopuses have superb night vision and long tentacles that they use to probe cracks in the reef, searching for food.

◄ Corals are nocturnal and are most active at night.

73 **Coral reef spiny lobsters march through the night.** At the end of the summer 100,000 of them set off on a long journey. Walking in single file towards deeper, darker water, they can travel up to 50 kilometres every night to reach their breeding grounds.

▼ A Christmas tree worm buries its body deep inside a coral. Only its two feeding tentacles, which look like trees, are visible.

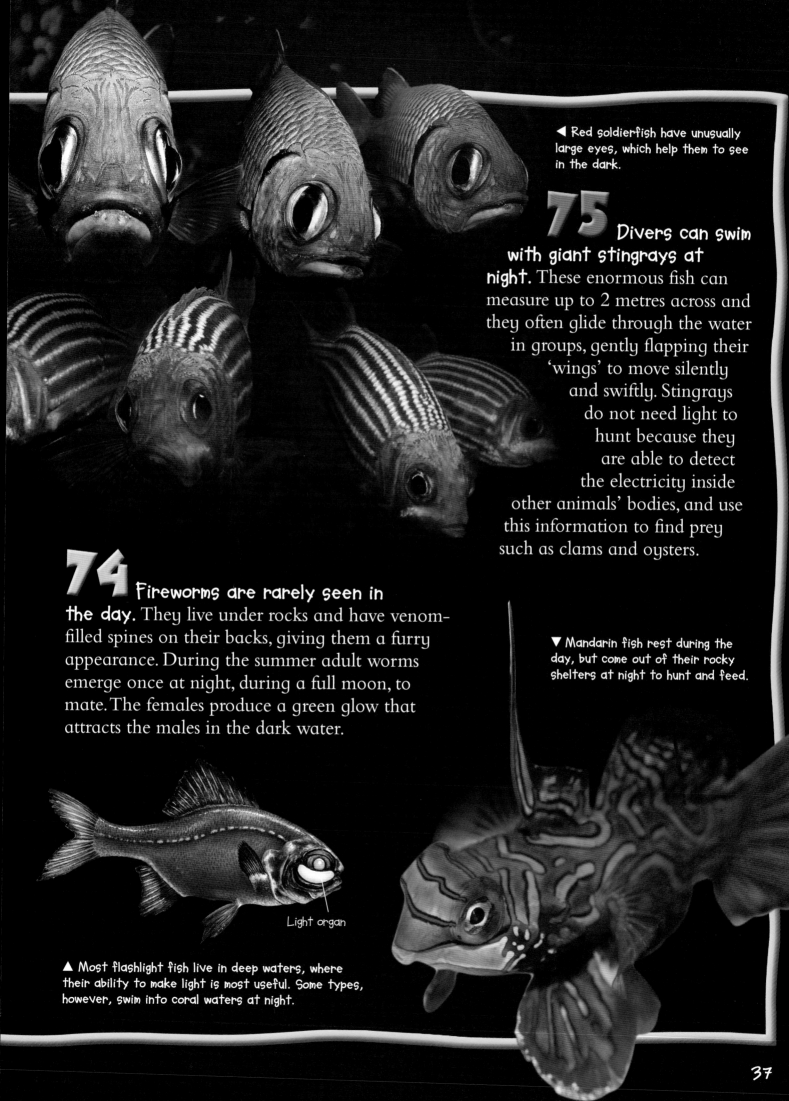

◄ Red soldierfish have unusually large eyes, which help them to see in the dark.

75 Divers can swim with giant stingrays at night. These enormous fish can measure up to 2 metres across and they often glide through the water in groups, gently flapping their 'wings' to move silently and swiftly. Stingrays do not need light to hunt because they are able to detect the electricity inside other animals' bodies, and use this information to find prey such as clams and oysters.

74 Fireworms are rarely seen in the day. They live under rocks and have venom-filled spines on their backs, giving them a furry appearance. During the summer adult worms emerge once at night, during a full moon, to mate. The females produce a green glow that attracts the males in the dark water.

▼ Mandarin fish rest during the day, but come out of their rocky shelters at night to hunt and feed.

Light organ

▲ Most flashlight fish live in deep waters, where their ability to make light is most useful. Some types, however, swim into coral waters at night.

Relying on reefs

76 Millions of people rely on coral reefs for their survival. These ecosystems not only support fish and other animals, they also protect coastal regions from damage by storms and wave action.

▲ The people from this fishing village in Borneo depend on the reef for food.

77 There are around 500 types of seaweeds living on the Great Barrier Reef alone. Seaweeds contain substances that are useful to humans. Agar comes from red seaweeds and is used to make desserts, or to thicken soups and ice-cream. Alginates come from brown seaweeds and they are used to make cosmetics, thicken drinks and in the manufacture of paper and textiles.

78 Ecosystems that have a large range of living things are often used in medical science. Many species of animals and plants that live on reefs are being used in the search for new medicines that will cure illnesses. Substances in coral polyps are being used to develop treatments for some diseases, and to help rebuild broken bones.

79 People who live around reefs have traded in coral products for thousands of years. The harvesting of red and pink corals for jewellery has caused many people to worry that the coral may be driven to extinction. Jewellery makers are asked to only use a small amount of coral every year and to only take coral from places where it will be protected as it regrows.

▶ Collecting food, such as fish, and precious coral is a traditional way to survive in many places where reefs grow.

80 Coral reefs help to support local communities through tourism. Millions of people flock to the world's reefs to enjoy nature's underwater spectacle. The money they spend there helps support local people, who provide accommodation, food and equipment. Reefs are worth much more alive than dead. While one shark could be killed and sold for food, it is worth at least one hundred times more alive as an attraction to reef tourists.

▼ A trained guide shows tourists the delights of the Great Barrier Reef. 'Ecotourism' allows visitors to enjoy the reef without damaging it.

QUIZ
What am I?
1. I am used to thicken ice cream and soups.
2. I travel and visit places of interest.
3. I grow on the reef and am often made into jewellery.

Answers:
1. Agar 2. Tourist
3. Red and pink coral

Underwater explorers

81 **Exploring a reef is a magical experience.** Bathed in warm, blue water, a diver can swim among thousands of fish that dart around the coral. As schools of small, silvery fish flash past, smaller groups of predator fish follow – fast and alert in the chase.

CREATE A CORAL

Use quick-dry clay to create your own corals, copying the pictures in this book to get the right shapes. Once dry, paint the corals in bright colours. You can also make fish or other wildlife, to build your own coral reef ecosystem.

82 **People have been fascinated by coral reefs for thousands of years.** They have enjoyed watching reef wildlife, but they have also explored in search of food and building materials. Since coral reefs grow in shallow, clear water swimmers can enjoy them without any special equipment. Snorkels allow swimmers to breathe while their faces are in water.

83 **The best way to explore a coral reef is to go underwater.** Scuba equipment allows a diver to swim and breathe below the water's surface. Using an oxygen tank, flippers and a face mask a diver can move carefully around a reef, watching the creatures or carrying out scientific studies.

▼ Special equipment allows divers to photograph underwater wildlife such as this Goliath grouper.

84 Scientists have been examining coral reefs for more than 300 years. There are many research centres and universities near large coral reefs, so scientists can collect information and learn about the reefs over many years. There are even underwater research laboratories, where scientists can study reefs close up for days at a time.

▼ Divers explore old reefs, but they also visit places where new reefs are forming on shipwrecks, to understand how they develop.

85 Exploring reefs is fascinating, but it can be dangerous too. Curious blacktip reef sharks may give a diver a warning nip, but a sting from a box jellyfish can be deadly. There are also poisonous sea snakes, octopuses, shellfish and fish.

Natural coral killers

86 Some fish not only live on a reef, they eat it too. There are more than 130 types of fish, known as corallivores, that feed on corals. They eat the slimy mucus made by polyps, the polyps themselves and even their stony cups. They like eating polyps during their breeding season because they are full of juicy, tasty eggs.

▼ Parrotfish change their appearance throughout their lives – they change colour as they grow up!

▲ Most coral-eating fish are butterfly fish. They have small mouths that can nibble at polyps and their eggs.

87 Reef-killing creatures have different eating habits around the world. In some regions, the coral-eating fish remove so much of the reef that it does not appear to grow at all. Threadfin butterfly fish in the Indian Ocean munch through large amounts of coral, but those that live around the Great Barrier Reef never eat coral. Corallivores that live in Caribbean reefs can survive on other food, too.

88 Parrotfish are dazzling in their appearance, but deadly in their lifestyle. They dig at coral with their tough mouths, which are like beaks, and grind it up in their throats. This releases the zooxanthellae that are an important part of their diet. The stony parts of the coral pass through their bodies, coming out the other end as beautiful white sand.

▲ Crown-of-thorns starfish graze on corals, especially in places where the starfish's natural enemy, the trumpet shellfish, has disappeared.

89 The crown-of-thorns starfish is one of the world's most famous coral-killers. It is covered in spines and can have as many as 21 'arms'. This starfish eats coral by turning its mouth inside out and pouring strong juices over the polyps to dissolve their flesh. It prefers fast-growing corals over the slower-growing types. The starfish eat the polyps, but leave the stony structure behind.

90 In the 1980s, Caribbean black sea urchins, called diademas, were wiped out by a deadly disease. These sea urchins kept the reefs healthy by grazing on seaweeds. Once they had died, seaweeds took over the coral, using up space and blocking out light. Seaweed-eating fish were also struggling to survive because too many of them had been caught by fishermen. There was nothing left to control the growth of seaweed and so the coral ecosystem was changed, and may never return to its previous, healthy state.

I DON'T BELIEVE IT!
Sponges are boring animals — they bore right into coral reefs! These simple animals dig right into the middle of a reef, making it weaker and more likely to collapse in storms.

Reefs at risk

91 Coral reefs are fragile ecosystems that are under threat from humans. When they are stressed, coral polyps lose their zooxanthellae, and die. Once the polyps have died the coral structure that is left appears white, and is described as 'bleached'.

▼ If zooxanthellae leave the coral, the polyps die. Over time, other types of algae and bacteria grow over the bleached coral.

1. Healthy coral with zooxanthellae living in coral tissue

2. Zooxanthellae leave coral due to increased water temperatures

3. Algae cover the damaged coral

▶ Global warming, a rise in worldwide temperatures, is caused by the polluting effects of carbon dioxide. It is raising sea temperatures and is causing coral bleaching.

92 Pollution, such as human waste (sewage) and chemicals used in farming, kills coral. In some places, pipes carry sewage to the sea where it mixes with the seawater. Sewage contains substances that feed seaweeds but bleach corals. On land, chemicals are used on crops to help them grow or to kill pests, but they get carried out to sea by rainwater and rivers, where they damage the reef and its inhabitants.

93 Damage to nearby land causes reefs to die. When coastal areas are changed by building or digging, soil is loosened and makes its way into the sea. Soil and dirt in seawater make it cloudy and stop sunlight from reaching the zooxanthellae. The result is more coral bleaching.

▶ Coral is broken up and taken from the sea to be used as a building material.

94 Catching and killing fish adds to the bleaching of coral reefs. In some parts of the world, fishermen use destructive methods of fishing. They drop bombs in the water, which explode and kill whole schools of fish, turning coral to crumbs. They also use chemicals, such as cyanide, to kill or stun fish.

95 Tourists enjoy reefs, but they also put them at risk. Visitors put pressure on local ecosystems because they need food, transport and places to stay – which means pollution, fishing and building. Some tourists damage reefs by standing on them or touching them, and by buying wildlife souvenirs such as coral jewellery.

SAVE OUR REEFS!
Make a poster to show the different ways coral reefs are being damaged and destroyed. Include a list of top tips for tourists to help them enjoy reefs safely without harming these ecosystems.

96 Saving our coral reefs is incredibly important. We need to protect them, or it is likely they will become the first major ecosystem to become extinct in modern times. Setting up national parks, and stopping all forms of fishing means that reefs can develop naturally.

97 Artificial reefs have been built to replace the natural ones that are under threat. Some man-made reefs have been successful but scientists now agree that saving the coral reefs we have is the best option. They are working to find new ways to save coral polyps and help them recover once their natural environment has been damaged.

98 All parts of a coral reef ecosystem need to be protected. Removing one part, such as a single type of fish, can have terrible effects on other animals and plants that live there. Supporting local people as they find alternative ways to make money and find food, rather than relying on reefs is an important step forward.

▼ To make an artificial reef, structures are placed on the seabed. Corals and other marine creatures settle here and start to create a new reef ecosystem.

99 The Komodo National Park in Indonesia covers 1817 square kilometres of land and sea. Tourists pay to support the workers and scientists who protect their natural environment, prevent illegal fishing and study the coral ecosystems in the park.

▲ Satellite photos of protected reefs, such as Hawaii's Pearl and Hermes atoll, help scientists find out how reefs are changing.

100 Scientists believe many coral reefs can be saved if they are protected now. Pollution is one of the biggest coral killers, and removing it could have an immediate effect on reefs' survival. This will give us more time to tackle the big problem of global warming, which will take many years.

▶ The ocean waters surrounding Komodo cover more than two-thirds of the National Park.

QUIZ

1. What do scientists believe could help save coral reefs?
2. Which word beginning with 'a' means man-made?
3. Why are national parks set up?

Answers:
1. Stopping pollution 2. Artificial 3. To protect endangered ecosystems

47

Index

Entries in **bold** refer to main subject entries. Entries in *italics* refer to illustrations.